Objection Overruled

The Ultimate Guide to Turning 'No' into 'Yes'"

Gerard Assey

Objection Overruled:

The Ultimate Guide to Turning 'No' into 'Yes'"

By

Gerard Assey

Published by:
Gerard Assey
19/18, Palli Arasan Street
Anna Nagar East
Chennai - 600 102

ISBN: 978-81-985691-4-1

Table of Contents

Preface

Sales is not just about pitching products or services—it's about solving problems, building relationships, and most importantly, overcoming resistance. Every salesperson, no matter how skilled, has encountered objections. Whether it's "It's too expensive," "We're happy with our current provider," or "We're not looking for a new solution right now," these statements can feel like roadblocks standing between you and the sale. But what if they weren't roadblocks at all? What if, instead of being obstacles, objections were actually opportunities—golden chances to engage, educate, and ultimately close the deal?

That's exactly what this book is about.

"Objection Overruled: *The Ultimate Guide to Turning 'No' into 'Yes'*" is designed to be your go-to handbook for handling objections with confidence, clarity, and strategy. Too often, salespeople see objections as rejection, when in reality, they are simply a buyer's way of expressing hesitation, uncertainty, or an unspoken need. The key to success is understanding what's really behind these objections and responding in a way that removes doubts, builds trust, and moves the conversation forward.

Having spent years studying top-performing sales professionals, I've observed one common trait among the best closers—they never back down from an objection. Instead, they embrace it, dig deeper, and turn it into a meaningful conversation that reinforces the value of their solution. This book will teach you how to do exactly that, using proven techniques, real-world examples, and step-by-step strategies that will help you handle any objection and close more sales.

What You'll Learn in This Book

- ✓ The psychology behind objections – Why do buyers push back, and how can you use that knowledge to your advantage?
- ✓ The most common objections in B2B sales – A detailed breakdown of objections and the best ways to handle them.
- ✓ The Four-Step Approach to Objection Handling – A systematic way to respond to any concern without sounding defensive or pushy.
- ✓ The power of storytelling, social proof, and negotiation – How to leverage testimonials, data, and case studies to neutralize resistance.
- ✓ Advanced objection-handling techniques – How to tailor responses for calls, emails, and in-person meetings.
- ✓ How to build long-term relationships – Because not every "No" is final, and sometimes a well-handled objection leads to future business.

Whether you're new to sales or a seasoned pro, this book will give you the tools to confidently handle objections and turn more conversations into closed deals.

Why This Book Matters Now More Than Ever

In today's competitive marketplace, buyers are more informed than ever. They have endless options, tight budgets, and less time to evaluate solutions. That means objections are more frequent and tougher to overcome. But instead of fearing them, the best salespeople welcome objections—because they know that every objection is an opportunity to differentiate, engage, and ultimately win.

Are you ready to become that kind of salesperson?

If so, let's begin. It's time to turn every "No" into "Yes" and overrule objections once and for all!

The Why, What & How of Objections

Why This Handbook? – The Importance of Mastering Objection Handling

Sales is often seen as a game of persuasion, but at its core, it is about solving problems and building trust. In the B2B sales environment, objections are inevitable. They are not merely obstacles but opportunities to deepen the conversation and uncover the real needs of a prospect. Yet, many sales professionals struggle with handling objections effectively. Some see them as rejections, while others respond defensively or give up too soon.

This handbook is designed to help sales professionals master the art of objection handling. It provides not just theoretical insights but practical, step-by-step methods to turn objections into opportunities. Mastering this skill can significantly improve sales conversions, strengthen customer relationships, and set a salesperson apart from the competition. Understanding and addressing objections effectively leads to smoother negotiations, shorter sales cycles, and greater customer confidence.

If sales were just about presenting a product or service, it would be easy. However, the real challenge lies in overcoming resistance and helping prospects see the value in what you offer. This handbook will equip you with the mindset, strategies, and techniques necessary to handle objections like a pro, transforming potential roadblocks into stepping stones for success.

What Are Sales Objections? – Definition and Common Misconceptions

A sales objection is any concern, hesitation, or reason a prospect gives for not proceeding with a purchase. These objections can range from pricing concerns to a lack of urgency, doubts about credibility, or even simple resistance to change. Every sales professional encounters them, and how they respond determines their success.

However, a common misconception is that an objection is the same as a rejection. This is not true. An objection is simply a sign that the prospect is not yet convinced or ready to move forward. In many cases, objections are actually buying signals—indications that the customer is interested but needs more information or reassurance. When handled properly, objections can lead to a stronger engagement, deeper trust, and ultimately, a successful sale.

Another misconception is that objections are always logical. In reality, many objections stem from emotional or psychological factors—fear of making the wrong decision, resistance to change, or loyalty to an existing vendor. Understanding this helps salespeople approach objections with empathy rather than frustration.

This handbook will help you distinguish between different types of objections, uncover the real reasons behind them, and respond in a way that reassures and persuades rather than pushes or pressures.

Why Do Customers Object? – Understanding the Psychology Behind Objections

To effectively handle objections, a salesperson must first understand why customers object in the first place. While objections may seem like direct challenges to a sale, they often stem from deeper concerns that are not always verbalized. Here are some psychological reasons why customers raise objections:

1. Fear of Making a Wrong Decision

Many B2B purchases involve significant financial and operational commitments. Decision-makers fear making a choice that could backfire. If they choose the wrong vendor or solution, it could negatively impact their company and even their own career. This fear often manifests as objections like “I need more time to decide” or “We are happy with our current vendor.”

2. Resistance to Change

Businesses, like individuals, are creatures of habit. Many companies prefer sticking to familiar processes and vendors rather than taking the risk of change. Even if your solution is better, a prospect might object simply because switching feels uncomfortable. This can result in objections like “We’ve always done it this way” or “It’s too complicated to switch.”

3. Budget Constraints or Perceived High Cost

Price-related objections are among the most common. However, the real issue is often not the price itself but the prospect’s perception of value. If they don’t see a clear return on investment (ROI), they will resist spending the money. That’s why they say things like “It’s too expensive” or “We don’t have the budget for this right now.”

4. Lack of Trust or Credibility

If a prospect is unfamiliar with your company, they might hesitate to commit. Businesses want to work with reliable partners, and if they have never heard of you, objections like "We prefer to work with established vendors" or "I've never heard of your company before" are common.

5. Lack of Urgency

If the problem your solution solves is not immediately painful for the prospect, they will postpone the decision. This is why salespeople often hear objections like "We'll look at this later" or "It's not a priority right now."

6. Lack of Decision-Making Power

Many times, the person you are speaking to does not have the final say. Instead of admitting this outright, they might say "I need to check with my boss" or "I'm not the right person to discuss this."

Understanding these psychological factors allows salespeople to go beyond surface-level objections and address the underlying concerns that prevent a sale from closing.

How Salespeople Typically React to Objections – Common Mistakes and Ineffective Responses

Objections are a natural part of the sales process, but many salespeople handle them poorly, which can result in lost deals. Here are some of the most common mistakes:

1. Becoming Defensive or Argumentative

Some salespeople see objections as personal rejections and react defensively. If a customer says "Your product is too expensive," an untrained salesperson might respond with "No, it's actually quite affordable compared to competitors." This response dismisses the customer's concern rather than addressing it. Instead of arguing, the salesperson should explore why the prospect feels that way and offer value-based reasoning.

2. Giving Up Too Quickly

Many sales professionals hear an objection and immediately assume the deal is dead. If a prospect says “We’re happy with our current vendor,” an inexperienced salesperson might say “Alright, thanks for your time” and end the conversation. However, skilled salespeople know that objections are opportunities to ask more questions and uncover the real concerns.

3. Talking Too Much Instead of Listening

A common mistake is bombarding the prospect with more information instead of listening to their concerns. For example, if a prospect objects due to budget constraints, an ineffective salesperson might start listing every feature instead of understanding the specific financial concerns.

4. Failing to Differentiate the Offer

Some salespeople respond to objections by simply repeating what the product does rather than explaining why it is unique or valuable. If a customer says “Your competitor offers a better price,” a poor response would be “Well, our product has great features too.” A stronger response would highlight unique differentiators that justify the cost.

5. Not Clarifying the Real Objection

Often, the first objection a prospect gives is not the real issue. If a customer says “I need more time,” it could mean they are not convinced about the value, they lack decision-making authority, or they genuinely have other priorities. A skilled salesperson probes further to uncover the true reason.

Handling objections effectively is a skill that separates top-performing sales professionals from the rest. This chapter has laid the foundation by helping you understand why objections occur, the psychology behind them, and common mistakes salespeople make. The next sections will dive into categorizing objections, step-by-step strategies to handle them, and how to turn objections into sales opportunities. Mastering this skill will not only increase your conversion rates but also establish stronger, trust-based relationships with your clients.

Types & Categories of Objections

In sales, objections are inevitable. However, they are not barriers; they are stepping stones to deeper conversations and better understanding. Every objection a potential client raises is an opportunity for a skilled salesperson to provide clarity, offer solutions, and build trust. This section explores the most common categories of objections encountered in B2B sales and provides insights into why they arise.

1. Price-Related Objections

Price is often the first and most frequent objection a salesperson encounters. It typically comes in statements like:

- ✓ *"Your solution is too expensive."*
- ✓ *"We don't have the budget for this."*
- ✓ *"I don't see the ROI on this investment."*

Understanding the Motive Behind Price Objections

Price objections usually stem from one of three core reasons:

- ✓ Budget constraints: The company genuinely does not have the financial resources allocated for the purchase.
- ✓ Perceived lack of value: The prospect does not see enough benefits to justify the cost.
- ✓ Comparison shopping: The buyer is benchmarking against competitors and believes they can get a better deal elsewhere.

Suggested Response to Price Objections

Instead of immediately offering a discount, sales professionals should shift the conversation from cost

to value. For example, if a prospect says, *"This is too expensive,"* a salesperson might respond:
"I understand that price is an important factor. Can I ask—what specific value are you looking for in a solution like ours? If we can demonstrate how this investment leads to measurable returns, would you be open to a discussion on how we can structure this to fit your budget?"
A practical exercise for sales teams is to prepare a 'Value vs. Price' matrix. In role-playing sessions, salespeople should practice demonstrating how the solution delivers ROI rather than focusing on the cost.

2. Value & Need-Based Objections
Sometimes, prospects claim they don't need the solution or are satisfied with their current vendor. Common statements include:

- ✓ *"We're happy with our current provider."*
- ✓ *"We don't see a need for this solution."*
- ✓ *"We handle this in-house."*

Understanding the Motive Behind These Objections
Such objections typically stem from:

- ✓ Lack of awareness: The customer may not fully understand how the solution benefits them.
- ✓ Complacency: The client is comfortable with their current vendor and doesn't see the need to change.
- ✓ Fear of change: Switching providers might seem like too much hassle.

Suggested Response to Value & Need-Based Objections

The key is to uncover pain points the prospect may not have considered. If a prospect says, *"We are happy with our current vendor,"* the salesperson could respond:

"That's great to hear. What aspects of their service do you find most valuable? Are there any areas where you think improvements could be made? Many of our clients initially felt the same but later realized there were gaps they hadn't considered. Can I share how we helped them optimize their process?"

3. Urgency-Based Objections

Prospects often defer decision-making with statements like:

- ✓ *"We're not looking at this right now."*
- ✓ *"We'll revisit this next quarter."*
- ✓ *"It's not a priority."*

Understanding the Motive Behind Urgency Objections

These objections usually arise due to:

- ✓ Lack of immediate pain: The customer does not feel an urgent need to solve the problem.
- ✓ Internal delays: The prospect might be waiting on approvals, funding, or project alignment.
- ✓ Procrastination: The decision-maker may be avoiding the hassle of change.

Suggested Response to Urgency-Based Objections

Instead of pressuring the client, a salesperson should create urgency by highlighting potential risks and missed opportunities. For example:

"I completely understand. That said, companies that delayed implementing this solution later faced [specific challenge]. Would you be open to exploring

how we can proactively address this now to avoid potential setbacks later?"

4. Authority & Decision-Making Objections

Prospects may push back by saying:

- ✓ *"I need to check with my boss."*
- ✓ *"I'm not the right person to decide."*

Understanding the Motive Behind Authority Objections

These objections arise when:

- ✓ The prospect lacks decision-making power: They may be an influencer rather than a final decision-maker.
- ✓ They are avoiding commitment: Some prospects use this as a polite way to disengage.

Suggested Response to Authority Objections

The goal is to identify the real decision-maker and secure a meeting. If a prospect says, "*I need to check with my boss,"* a good response would be:

"I completely understand. Would it be helpful if we arranged a brief call with them so I can directly address any questions they might have? I'd love to ensure they have all the information needed to make an informed decision."

5. Trust & Confidence-Based Objections

Some prospects hesitate due to concerns like:

- ✓ *"I've never heard of your company before."*
- ✓ *"We had a bad experience with a similar product."*

Understanding the Motive Behind Trust-Based Objections

These objections arise when:

- ✓ The prospect is unfamiliar with the company.

- ✓ They had negative past experiences with similar vendors.
- ✓ They fear making a mistake.

Suggested Response to Trust-Based Objections

Building trust takes credibility and reassurance. If a prospect is skeptical, a salesperson could say:

"I completely understand. In fact, many of our best customers felt the same way initially. Would it be helpful if I shared some case studies or connected you with a client who had similar concerns but saw great results with us?"

6. Process & Implementation Objections

Some prospects are reluctant to change because of logistical concerns:

- ✓ *"It's too difficult to switch vendors."*
- ✓ *"We are locked into a contract."*
- ✓ *"Integration with our current system will be too complex."*

Understanding the Motive Behind Process Objections

These concerns arise when:

- ✓ The prospect fears a disruptive transition.
- ✓ They have contractual limitations.
- ✓ They perceive integration as a hassle.

Suggested Response to Process-Based Objections

The key is to simplify the process and remove perceived obstacles. A salesperson might respond:

"I understand that switching providers can seem challenging. We have a dedicated onboarding team that ensures a seamless transition with minimal disruption. Can I walk you through how this would work step-by-step?"

The Professional Way to Handle Objections

Developing the Right Mindset for Handling Objections

Sales objections are a natural part of the selling process. Many sales professionals, especially those new to B2B sales, see objections as rejection or failure. However, seasoned professionals understand that objections are simply opportunities in disguise. An objection means the prospect is engaged in the conversation. If they weren't interested, they would simply say, "No, thanks," and walk away.

The key to handling objections successfully begins with your mindset. You must train yourself to remain calm, confident, and positive when faced with resistance. Instead of reacting with frustration or defensiveness, approach objections with curiosity. Every objection is a window into your prospect's thoughts, concerns, and priorities.

Imagine two salespeople in a meeting:

The first salesperson, upon hearing, "Your price is too high," immediately jumps into defensive mode, saying, "Well, that's the cost of quality!" The prospect shuts down. The conversation is over.

The second salesperson, upon hearing the same objection, smiles and calmly asks, "I understand. Could you share more about what you were expecting in terms of price versus value?" This opens the door to discussion, understanding, and negotiation.

This is the power of mindset. Instead of seeing objections as obstacles, see them as opportunities to educate, engage, and guide.

Exercise: Mindset Shift Practice

Write down three common objections you face in your sales process. Next to each, write your immediate reaction. Then, rewrite the response in a way that shows curiosity and calmness instead of defensiveness.

The Four-Step Approach to Handling Objections

There is a structured way to handle objections that ensures you stay in control of the conversation while also making the prospect feel heard. The four-step method involves:

1. Acknowledge & Empathize

The worst thing a salesperson can do when faced with an objection is dismiss it outright. If a prospect says, "This is too expensive," and you respond with, "No, it's not! It's actually very affordable," you have invalidated their concern and likely lost the sale.

Instead, acknowledge their concern and show empathy. Saying something like, "I completely understand that pricing is an important factor. Many of our customers initially had similar concerns," helps the prospect feel validated. When people feel heard, they become more open to discussion.

Example:

Prospect: *"We're happy with our current vendor."*

Bad Response: *"They're not as good as us! We offer better service."*

Good Response: *"I totally understand. Loyalty is important in business. May I ask what you value most in your current vendor?"*

This approach keeps the conversation going instead of creating resistance.

2. Ask & Clarify

Many objections aren't what they seem on the surface. If a prospect says, "*We don't have the budget,*" it may not be a lack of money—it could mean they don't see enough value in what you're offering.

Instead of taking objections at face value, ask clarifying questions to get to the real issue. Some good probing questions include:

"When you say the price is too high, do you mean it's outside your budget for this quarter, or do you mean you don't see the ROI?"

"If price weren't a concern, would this solution otherwise meet your needs?"

"Can you share what specifically makes you hesitant about moving forward?"

The goal is to dig deeper and uncover the true motivation behind the objection.

Example:

Prospect: *"We need to think about it."*

Clarifying Response: "I completely understand. When you say 'think about it,' are there specific concerns you need to address internally?"

3. Address with Value

Once you've clarified the real concern, you can provide a response that aligns with their needs. This isn't about arguing or forcing the sale—it's about helping the prospect see the true value of your solution.

If the issue is price, explain the ROI (return on investment). If they are worried about switching from a current vendor, offer a smooth transition plan. If they are hesitant about timing, show them the risks of delaying the decision.

Example:
Prospect: *"Your product costs 20% more than our current solution."*
Value-Based Response: *"I understand why that's a concern. What we've seen with clients in similar situations is that while the upfront cost is higher, they actually save money long-term because of our lower maintenance costs and higher efficiency. Over a year, this could lead to a 15% overall cost reduction. Would you like me to break down how that works?"*
Instead of justifying the price, you shift the conversation to value.

4. Confirm & Move Forward
Once you've addressed the concern, don't stop there. Many salespeople make the mistake of handling the objection but then failing to guide the conversation toward a next step. Always confirm and ask for commitment.
Example:
Prospect: *"I need to talk to my team before making a decision."*
Follow-Up: "That makes sense. Would it be helpful if I provided a summary document with key benefits and pricing details for your internal discussion? Also, can we schedule a follow-up call for next Tuesday to go over any questions that come up?"
This keeps the deal moving instead of letting it fade away.

Exercise: The Objection Handling Role-Play
Pair up with a colleague and take turns presenting objections and responding using the four-step approach. The goal is to remain calm, ask clarifying questions, and respond with value.

Common Mistakes in Objection Handling

Many sales professionals struggle with objections because they:

- ✓ Get Defensive – Arguing with the prospect instead of listening.
- ✓ Accept Objections at Face Value – Not probing deeper to find the true reason.
- ✓ Overload with Information – Trying to solve the objection by dumping too much information.
- ✓ Fail to Follow Up – Leaving the conversation without a next step.

By avoiding these mistakes and using the four-step framework, sales professionals can handle objections with confidence and effectiveness.

The Role of Storytelling in Overcoming Objections

People remember stories more than facts. When a prospect raises an objection, one of the most powerful ways to respond is by sharing a success story about another customer who had the same concern but achieved great results.

For example, if a prospect says, *"Switching vendors is too complicated,"* you can respond with:

"I understand completely. One of our clients, XYZ Corp, felt the same way. They had been with their old vendor for ten years and were worried about disruptions. However, we worked closely with their team, handled the entire transition, and within a month, they were up and running smoothly. Now, they save 20% on costs and are much happier with our service."

This makes the response relatable and convincing.

Exercise: Storytelling Practice

Write down three common objections you face and develop a real customer story to address each.

When to Walk Away

Not every objection can or should be overcome. Some prospects will never buy because:

- ✓ They truly don't need your solution.
- ✓ They lack decision-making power or funds.
- ✓ They are just gathering information with no real intent to buy.

If you've clarified, addressed concerns, and still sense resistance, it may be best to move on and focus on better opportunities.

Objection handling is not about arguing or convincing—it's about understanding, clarifying, and guiding. By staying calm, asking the right questions, and presenting value, sales professionals can turn objections into successful deals.

Master List of 30 Most Common B2B Sales Objections & How to Handle Them.

Here are the top 30 sales objections commonly faced by sales personnel in a B2B environment, expressed as customers would say them:

1. "We're happy with our current vendor."
2. "It's too expensive."
3. "We don't have the budget for this right now."
4. "We're not looking for a new solution."
5. "I need to check with my boss/decision-maker."
6. "We've tried something similar before, and it didn't work."
7. "There's no urgent need for this at the moment."
8. "Can you send me an email? I'll get back to you later."
9. "We're in the middle of another project right now."
10. "We don't see the ROI in this."
11. "Your competitor is offering a better price."
12. "We're locked into a contract with another supplier."
13. "We don't have time to implement this right now."
14. "Your product/service doesn't meet our specific needs."
15. "We prefer to build an in-house solution instead."
16. "I don't see how this will benefit our company."
17. "It's too complicated to switch providers."

18. “I’ve never heard of your company before.”
19. “How do I know this will actually work for us?”
20. “This isn’t a priority for us at the moment.”
21. “Your solution doesn’t integrate with our current systems.”
22. “We’ve already allocated our budget for the year.”
23. “I’m not the right person to discuss this.”
24. “We need more time to evaluate our options.”
25. “Our company doesn’t make quick decisions.”
26. “We’re waiting for approval from higher-ups.”
27. “We had a bad experience with a similar product before.”
28. “We don’t see a big enough problem to justify this purchase.”
29. “Your company is too new; we prefer established vendors.”
30. “We’re not sure your company will be around long-term.”

We will now handle these 30 most common objections listed above in B2B sales, breaking them down using the **four-step approach** outlined in the previous chapter. The goal is not just to provide scripted responses but to help you- the sales professional understand the psychology behind each objection and respond with confidence, logic, and value.

Objection #1: ***“We’re happy with our current vendor.”***

Motive Behind It:

When a prospect says they are happy with their current vendor, they are often expressing one or more of the following concerns:

- ✓ They fear disrupting an established relationship that seems to be working fine.
- ✓ They feel a sense of loyalty to their current provider and don't want to risk change.
- ✓ They might not see enough difference between your solution and their existing one.
- ✓ They might be using this as a polite way to shut down the conversation.

While this objection can feel like a dead end, it's actually a golden opportunity to explore gaps, differentiate your offering, and position your solution as the superior choice.

Handling This Objection Using the Four-Step Approach

Step 1: Acknowledge & Empathize

A defensive response like *"But we offer a much better service!"* will immediately put the prospect on guard. Instead, begin by acknowledging their satisfaction and showing respect for their existing relationship**.**

Example:

"That makes perfect sense. It's always great to hear that a company is happy with its current vendor. Long-term relationships in business are valuable, and I respect that. Many of our customers actually felt the same way before they switched to us."

This statement reassures the prospect that you are not here to attack their decision but to explore possibilities.

Step 2: Ask & Clarify

The key is to gently uncover any frustrations or gaps that may exist without the prospect even realizing it. Instead of bluntly asking, *"What do you dislike about your vendor?"* try a softer approach:

"Out of curiosity, what do you like most about your current vendor? And if you could improve one thing about the service, what would it be?"

This question subtly encourages them to reflect on potential pain points.

If they say, *"Everything is fine,"* dig a little deeper:

"I understand. If you ever had to explore alternatives in the future, what would be the most important factors in making that decision?"

This helps you uncover their real priorities and position your solution accordingly.

Step 3: Address with Value

Now that you understand what they value and where they see room for improvement, you can position your offering accordingly. If they expressed any frustrations with their current provider, this is your chance to address them.

Example:

"One thing our clients often mention is that they didn't realize how much time and cost they were losing with their previous vendor until they experienced our streamlined process. We actually helped [Client X] reduce their turnaround time by 30% while maintaining the same budget. I'd love to explore whether we could bring similar efficiency to your operations."

Here, you are not attacking their vendor but showing a compelling reason to consider a switch.

Step 4: Confirm & Move Forward

Instead of pushing for an immediate change, invite them to explore your offering without pressure:

"I'm not here to force a decision today, but would you be open to a quick side-by-side comparison of how our solution stacks up? If nothing else, it could serve as a benchmark for the future."

This keeps the door open for future discussions and moves the conversation forward.

Exercise: Vendor Loyalty Reflection

Think about a time when you stuck with a service provider out of habit or loyalty. What finally made you switch? Write down two ways you could use that reasoning in a sales conversation.

Objection #2: *"It's too expensive."*

Motive Behind It:

When a prospect objects to the price, they are not necessarily saying they cannot afford it. Instead, they might mean:

- ✓ They don't see enough value to justify the price.
- ✓ They are comparing you to a cheaper alternative.
- ✓ They are price-shopping to negotiate a better deal.
- ✓ They simply weren't expecting the cost to be that high.

The key to handling this objection is not defending the price, but rather shifting the focus to value.

Handling This Objection Using the Four-Step Approach

Step 1: Acknowledge & Empathize

Responding with *"No, we're actually very affordable!"* can feel dismissive. Instead, acknowledge their concern and open the conversation.

Example:

"I completely understand. Budget is always a key factor in any decision. Many of our customers initially felt the same way before they saw how much value they gained over time."

This reassures them that their concern is valid while leaving room for discussion.

Step 2: Ask & Clarify

Rather than assuming price is the only issue, probe deeper. Ask questions to uncover the real hesitation.

Example:

"When you say 'too expensive,' do you mean it's over your budget for this quarter, or do you mean you're not seeing the value at this price point?"

If they say it's a budget issue, you can explore payment options. If they say they don't see the value, you can emphasize ROI and benefits.

Step 3: Address with Value

If the objection is about value, shift the focus to the ROI.

Example:

"I understand that our price is higher than some competitors, but let's look at what that extra investment gets you. Over three years, our solution saves companies an average of 25% in operational costs. That means you're actually spending less in the long run. Would you like me to walk you through how that works?"

If the objection is about budget, offer flexible solutions.

Example:

"I hear you. We do offer flexible payment structures that can help spread out the investment. Would it be helpful if I outlined some options that might fit within your financial planning?"

Step 4: Confirm & Move Forward

To keep the conversation going, ask for a next step.

Example:

"Would you be open to a quick ROI breakdown to see if the long-term savings justify the investment?"

By shifting from cost to value, you help the prospect see why your solution is worth it.

Exercise: Price vs. Value Case Study

Think of a time when you bought a higher-priced product because it offered better value. How did you justify it? Write a short explanation that you could adapt for sales conversations.

Objection #3: *"We don't have the budget for this right now."*

Motive Behind It:

This objection often means:

- ✓ The company is in a tight financial period.
- ✓ The decision-maker is prioritizing other investments.
- ✓ The ROI is unclear, so they don't want to allocate funds.

The key here is to explore timing, payment flexibility, and ROI.

Handling This Objection Using the Four-Step Approach

Step 1: Acknowledge & Empathize

"I completely understand—budgets are always tight, and timing is key in any investment decision."

Step 2: Ask & Clarify

"Is the budget concern due to a company-wide freeze, or is it about prioritizing other projects right now?"

This helps determine whether the issue is temporary or a real roadblock.

Step 3: Address with Value

If the issue is timing, offer a future plan:

"Would it make sense to revisit this next quarter? I can follow up when budgets are being reassessed."

If the issue is ROI, provide a case study:
"One of our clients had similar budget concerns but saved 30% on costs within six months. Would you be open to seeing how this could work for you?"
Step 4: Confirm & Move Forward
"Would a cost-benefit analysis help in planning for future investment?"
This keeps the conversation alive without pushing for an immediate sale.

Objection #4: *"We're not looking for a new solution."*
Motive Behind It:
This objection is often a knee-jerk reaction from prospects who:

- ✓ *Are content with their current processes and see no reason to change.*
- ✓ *Feel overwhelmed with other priorities and don't want to explore new options.*
- ✓ *Assume that switching to a new solution is too complicated or unnecessary.*
- ✓ *Want to avoid a sales conversation and are using this as a polite rejection.*

Handling This Objection Using the Four-Step Approach
Step 1: Acknowledge & Empathize
The worst response to this objection is to immediately argue or push back. Instead, the key is to acknowledge their position while keeping the door open for conversation.
"I completely understand. Many of our clients felt the same way at first—they weren't actively looking for a new solution either. They were busy managing their current systems and didn't see an immediate reason

to change. But once they realized what they were missing, they were glad they took a closer look."

This response removes pressure and reassures them that their reaction is normal.

Step 2: Ask & Clarify

To uncover their real reason for saying this, ask a question that invites discussion.

"Just out of curiosity, what's working well for you right now that makes you feel you don't need a new solution?"

If they respond positively about their current setup, follow up with:

"That's great to hear. And if you could improve one thing in your current process, what would it be?"

This helps them identify potential pain points that they may not have considered before.

Step 3: Address with Value

Once you identify a possible area for improvement, position your solution as something worth exploring, rather than an immediate purchase.

"One of the biggest things our clients tell us is that they didn't realize how much inefficiency they were dealing with until they saw a side-by-side comparison. Would it be worth 15 minutes to see if there's an opportunity for you to save time or reduce costs?"

This approach lowers resistance because you're not asking them to switch today—just to explore.

Step 4: Confirm & Move Forward

Instead of pushing for a sale, keep the door open.

"Would it make sense to do a quick comparison next week? No pressure—just a chance to see if there's untapped potential for improvement."

This removes commitment pressure and makes them more likely to say yes.

Exercise: Identifying Hidden Pain Points

List three reasons a company might initially say they don't need a new solution. Then, write three follow-up questions that could help uncover hidden inefficiencies they might not have considered.

Objection #5: *"I need to check with my boss/decision-maker."*

Motive Behind It:

When a prospect says they need to check with someone else, they may actually be:

- ✓ Stalling because they're not interested but don't want to say no.
- ✓ Unsure if they have the authority to make the decision.
- ✓ Genuinely needing approval from a senior decision-maker.

The key is to understand whether they are a true influencer in the decision-making process and how to move the deal forward.

Handling This Objection Using the Four-Step Approach

Step 1: Acknowledge & Empathize

Show that you understand their position instead of trying to bypass them.

"That makes perfect sense. Most companies have multiple stakeholders involved in these decisions, and I completely respect that."

Step 2: Ask & Clarify

Determine whether they truly need approval or are just trying to end the conversation.

"Just so I understand, what's the process for getting approval on solutions like this in your company?"

If they hesitate or seem unsure, it may mean they lack influence in the decision. If they give a clear answer, it indicates they truly need to consult someone else.

Step 3: Address with Value

If they are a true influencer, equip them with the right information:

"Since your boss will likely ask about ROI and implementation, would it be helpful if I provided a summary you can share with them?"

If they are not the right person, try to involve the decision-maker directly:

"Would it be useful if we set up a quick call with them together so they can ask any questions upfront?"

This helps you stay in control of the conversation instead of waiting passively for a response.

Step 4: Confirm & Move Forward

Instead of leaving it open-ended, set a clear next step:

"When do you expect to discuss this with them? Would it make sense for me to follow up afterward to answer any remaining questions?"

This keeps the conversation active instead of fading into uncertainty.

Exercise: Mapping the Decision-Making Process

Think about a recent sale where a prospect needed approval. Write down three ways you could have helped speed up the decision process.

Objection #6: *"We've tried something similar before, and it didn't work."*

Motive Behind It:

This objection usually comes from past disappointment, meaning:

- ✓ *They had a bad experience with a similar product.*
- ✓ *They invested money but didn't see results.*
- ✓ *They are skeptical about making the same mistake again.*

The key is to differentiate your solution from their past experience.

Handling This Objection Using the Four-Step Approach

Step 1: Acknowledge & Empathize

"I completely understand. No one wants to repeat a mistake, and I respect that you're being cautious."

Step 2: Ask & Clarify

"Just so I can understand, what specifically didn't work last time? Was it the implementation, the support, or the results?"

This helps pinpoint the real issue.

Step 3: Address with Value

Once you understand the problem, explain how your solution is different:

"That makes sense. A big difference with our approach is that we provide dedicated on-boarding support, so you're not left figuring things out alone. In fact, [Client X] had a similar past experience but saw a 40% improvement after working with us."

Step 4: Confirm & Move Forward

"Would you be open to a short demo to see exactly how we prevent those issues?"

This keeps the conversation open without forcing a commitment.

Objection #7: *"There's no urgent need for this at the moment."*

Motive Behind It:

The prospect does not see an immediate benefit, often because:

- ✓ *They don't perceive the problem as pressing.*
- ✓ *They are focused on short-term priorities.*
- ✓ *The best response is to create a sense of urgency.*

Suggested Response

"I understand. Many businesses delay decisions until something becomes a major issue. What we often find is that companies who act early gain a competitive edge while others scramble to catch up. Would it be worth exploring if this could help you now rather than when it becomes urgent?"

Objection #8: *"Can you send me an email? I'll get back to you later."*

Suggested Response

"I'd be happy to send you some details, but just so I don't overwhelm you, what specifically would be most useful to include?"

This forces them to engage rather than brushing you off.

Objection #9: *"We're in the middle of another project right now."*

Motive Behind It:

This objection is typically a delaying tactic rather than a firm rejection. It may stem from:

- ✓ *A genuine focus on an important project, making them hesitant to take on anything new.*
- ✓ *A lack of urgency, where they don't yet see the value in prioritizing your solution.*
- ✓ *A polite way to brush off the conversation without outright rejecting you.*

Handling This Objection Using the Four-Step Approach

Step 1: Acknowledge & Empathize

A dismissive response would push the prospect further away. Instead, showing understanding helps build trust.

"I completely understand. Timing is crucial, and managing multiple projects at once can be overwhelming. Many of our clients have been in the same situation, and I respect that you need to stay focused."

This validates their concern rather than pushing against it.

Step 2: Ask & Clarify

Before assuming they're not interested, it's essential to dig deeper and determine if their objection is based on priority or a lack of perceived value.

"Just so I understand, when would be a better time to revisit this conversation? Is it about bandwidth right now, or are there other concerns regarding fit or value?"

If they mention a specific timeline, you can follow up accordingly. If they hesitate or don't give a clear answer, it may indicate a lack of real interest.

Step 3: Address with Value

To prevent the deal from getting stalled indefinitely, offer a way to make the decision easier without adding extra work for them.

"One thing that's helped our clients in similar situations is taking 15 minutes now to explore how this fits into their long-term strategy. That way, when things slow down, you're already ahead of the game. Would it be worth setting up a short discussion to explore the potential impact?"

This approach minimizes perceived effort and makes it easier for them to say yes.

Step 4: Confirm & Move Forward

Rather than leaving the conversation open-ended, secure a next step.

"Would it make sense to check in after your current project wraps up? I can send over some key insights now so you have everything ready when the timing is better."

By keeping the conversation active, you avoid getting permanently pushed aside.

Exercise: Understanding Timing Concerns

Write down three reasons a prospect might genuinely delay a decision. Then, craft three responses that help position your solution as a strategic, rather than disruptive, investment.

Objection #10: *"We don't see the ROI in this."*

Motive Behind It:

This objection typically arises when:

- ✓ *The prospect doesn't yet understand the financial benefits of your solution.*
- ✓ *They are focused on cost rather than long-term value.*
- ✓ *They have been burned by a past investment that didn't deliver results.*

Handling This Objection Using the Four-Step Approach

Step 1: Acknowledge & Empathize

No one wants to spend money without seeing a clear return. Acknowledge their concern to show that you're on the same page.

"That's a completely fair point. Every business wants to ensure they're making investments that generate real returns. I'd feel the same way in your position."

Step 2: Ask & Clarify

Rather than immediately pushing ROI calculations, first understand what ROI means to them.

"When you say you don't see the ROI, do you mean in terms of direct cost savings, increased efficiency, or something else?"

This helps uncover what they actually value. If they care about efficiency, showing cost savings won't be as effective as demonstrating time savings.

Step 3: Address with Value

Once you know their key concern, tailor your response to show real, tangible benefits.

"That makes sense. For companies similar to yours, our solution has helped reduce process inefficiencies by 30%, saving an average of 20 hours per month per employee. Over a year, that's a significant cost saving. Would it help if I shared a case study on how we achieved this?"

This makes ROI real rather than theoretical.

Step 4: Confirm & Move Forward

Instead of forcing them to accept your point, give them an easy way to explore further.

"Would it make sense to schedule a short session where I can show you real numbers based on your industry data?"

Exercise: Demonstrating ROI

Choose a product or service you sell. Create a simple case study showing tangible ROI figures and practice presenting it convincingly.

Objection #11: *"Your competitor is offering a better price."*

Motive Behind It:

Price objections often indicate:

- ✓ A focus on cost over value.
- ✓ A negotiation tactic to get a better deal.
- ✓ A misunderstanding of the unique advantages of your solution.

Handling This Objection Using the Four-Step Approach

Step 1: Acknowledge & Empathize

"I completely understand—pricing is always an important consideration. If I were in your shoes, I'd want to ensure I was getting the best deal too."

Step 2: Ask & Clarify

Instead of immediately offering a discount, understand what "better price" means.

"Just so I understand, what aspects of their offer stand out to you the most? Is it purely cost, or are there additional factors involved?"

If they only mention price, you know the objection is negotiable. If they mention additional benefits, you may need to address those as well.

Step 3: Address with Value

Rather than competing on price alone, highlight unique differentiators.

"What our clients have found is that while some competitors may offer a lower initial price, our solution delivers greater long-term savings through efficiency, support, and scalability. Would you like a side-by-side comparison to see the bigger picture?"

Step 4: Confirm & Move Forward

"If price is the main concern, let's discuss ways to make this work within your budget while ensuring you

get the best value. Can we explore some flexible options?"

Exercise: Differentiating Beyond Price
List three key advantages your product has over competitors and create a scripted response to justify your pricing based on value.

Objection #12: *"We're locked into a contract with another supplier."*
Suggested Response
"That makes sense. Many of our best clients were in long-term contracts when we first spoke. What we found is that it's never too early to explore options for when your contract is up. Would it be helpful to see how we compare, so when the time comes, you already have a clear alternative?"
This keeps the conversation open without pushing them to break a contract.

Objection #13: *"We don't have time to implement this right now."*
Suggested Response
"I completely get that. Implementation can seem like a big commitment. One thing that's helped our clients is our streamlined onboarding process, which takes only [X] hours. Would it be worth a quick chat to see if we can make it work within your current schedule?"
This removes the fear of complexity and opens the door to further discussion.

Objection #14: *"Your product/service doesn't meet our specific needs."*
Motive Behind It:

This objection usually arises when a prospect believes that your solution does not align with their business requirements. The reasons behind this perception can vary:

- ✓ *They may not fully understand how your product/service can be customized or adapted to their needs.*
- ✓ *They might have been misinformed about the capabilities of your solution.*
- ✓ *They could be comparing your solution to a competitor's offering and assuming it lacks critical features.*

Handling This Objection Using the Four-Step Approach

Step 1: Acknowledge & Empathize

It's important to validate the prospect's concern instead of dismissing it. A response like:

"I completely understand. Every company has unique challenges, and it's important to ensure that any solution aligns with your specific requirements. Many of our clients initially felt the same way."

This acknowledgment prevents the conversation from turning into a debate.

Step 2: Ask & Clarify

The next step is to uncover the specific need they believe your solution doesn't meet. Asking a targeted question can help:

"Just so I understand better, which particular needs do you feel aren't covered by our solution?"

Depending on their response, you might find that:

- ✓ They misunderstood a feature.
- ✓ They are comparing you unfairly with a competitor.

- ✓ They have an actual need your product doesn't cover (in which case, you must be honest).

Step 3: Address with Value

If your product does cover their need but they don't see it, now is the time to clarify:

"That makes sense. In fact, many of our clients had similar concerns initially. However, our solution does include [feature], which addresses [specific problem]. Would it help if I showed you exactly how that works?"

If your solution doesn't fully meet their need, explore if there's a workaround:

"I see where you're coming from. While our product doesn't directly offer [specific feature], many of our clients have successfully integrated it with [complementary tool]. Would you be open to discussing how this could still work for you?"

Step 4: Confirm & Move Forward

Once the value is established, solidify the next step:

"Would it be useful if I arranged a quick demo focused on this particular concern? That way, you can see exactly how it aligns with your needs."

This keeps the conversation moving and prevents the objection from becoming a roadblock.

Exercise: Identifying Feature Gaps

Write down three features of your product/service that clients often misunderstand or underutilize. Develop a short explanation for each, showing how they solve specific business needs.

Objection #15: *"We prefer to build an in-house solution instead."*

Motive Behind It:

This objection is common when prospects believe that:

- ✓ They have the resources to create a similar solution internally.
- ✓ They want complete control over the system, rather than relying on an external vendor.
- ✓ They assume building in-house will be more cost-effective in the long run.

Handling This Objection Using the Four-Step Approach

Step 1: Acknowledge & Empathize

Respect their preference while keeping the conversation open:

"That makes sense. Many companies explore in-house options first, especially when they want complete control over the solution. That's a logical approach."

Step 2: Ask & Clarify

Understand their reasoning for wanting to develop internally:

"Out of curiosity, what's driving the decision to build rather than buy? Is it cost, customization, or integration with existing systems?"

Their response will guide your next step. If it's cost, you can compare the long-term expenses of maintenance. If it's customization, highlight your solution's flexibility.

Step 3: Address with Value

"Building in-house definitely gives you control, but it also comes with ongoing maintenance costs, development delays, and resource allocation challenges. Many companies find that an external solution offers the same flexibility at a fraction of the time and cost. Would you be open to discussing how our solution might save you those headaches?"

Step 4: Confirm & Move Forward
Suggest a discussion to compare options:
"How about we do a side-by-side comparison of costs and timeframes? That way, you can make the best decision with all the information."

Objection #16: ***"I don't see how this will benefit our company."***
Motive Behind It:
This indicates a lack of perceived value. The prospect either:

- ✓ *Doesn't understand how your product solves a specific pain point.*
- ✓ *Doesn't see enough differentiation from their current process.*
- ✓ *Hasn't experienced enough of the problem to feel urgency.*

Handling This Objection Using the Four-Step Approach
Step 1: Acknowledge & Empathize
"I completely get that. If I didn't see clear benefits, I wouldn't move forward either."
Step 2: Ask & Clarify
"What's your top priority right now? Understanding that will help me see if this solution fits or not."
Step 3: Address with Value
Tie your solution directly to their goals:
"Since your priority is [X], here's how our solution directly impacts that. For example, we helped [Client] achieve [specific measurable result]. Would you like to explore how this applies to you?"
Step 4: Confirm & Move Forward
"Would it make sense to do a brief session where I can map out how this aligns with your company's needs?"

Objection #17: *"It's too complicated to switch providers."*

Motive Behind It:

Prospects worry about:

- ✓ *The disruption of migrating to a new solution.*
- ✓ *The effort required for onboarding.*
- ✓ *Hidden costs of switching.*

Handling This Objection Using the Four-Step Approach

Acknowledge their concern and highlight ease of transition:

"That's a completely valid concern. Switching providers can feel overwhelming, and minimizing disruption is key."

"Many of our clients felt the same way until they saw how streamlined our onboarding process is. We provide dedicated support, data migration, and hands-on training to make the transition seamless."

"Would it be helpful if I walked you through our step-by-step migration plan?"

Objection #18: *"I've never heard of your company before."*

Motive Behind It:

The prospect lacks familiarity and trust.

Handling This Objection Using the Four-Step Approach

Acknowledge and position it as an opportunity:

"That's fair. Many of our best clients started in the same position. Would it help if I shared a few success stories and client testimonials?"

Use social proof to build credibility:

"For example, [Company] had never worked with us before, but within six months, they saw a [specific

result]. I'd be happy to connect you with a client who was in the same position you are now."
Confirm the next step:
"Would it make sense to set up a quick introduction call where I can provide more background on how we've helped companies like yours?"

Objection #19: *"How do I know this will actually work for us?"*
Motive Behind It:
This objection is driven by doubt and risk aversion. The prospect is unsure whether your solution will deliver the promised results in their specific business environment. This hesitation can stem from:

- ✓ *Lack of familiarity with your product or company.*
- ✓ *A bad experience with a similar solution in the past.*
- ✓ *Concern about wasting time, money, or resources on an unproven solution.*

Handling This Objection Using the Four-Step Approach
Step 1: Acknowledge & Empathize
It's important to reassure the prospect that their concern is valid. Dismissing their doubt outright can make them defensive.
"That's a great question, and I completely understand why you'd want to be sure before making a decision. No company wants to invest in something that won't deliver results."
Step 2: Ask & Clarify
The goal here is to understand the specific doubts they have. Asking the right question can uncover what's really holding them back.

"Are there particular aspects of our solution that you're unsure about? Are you concerned about implementation, results, or something else?"

Depending on their response, you can tailor your approach. For instance, if they're worried about measurable results, focus on case studies. If they fear integration issues, highlight customer success stories.

Step 3: Address with Value

This is where you provide proof. Share relevant case studies, testimonials, or data points that show real-world success.

"Many of our clients had the same concern before they worked with us. One company, [Client Name], had similar challenges, and within [timeframe], they saw [specific benefit]. Would it help if I showed you the details of their journey?"

If available, offering a risk-free trial or a performance-based agreement can ease their hesitation.

Step 4: Confirm & Move Forward

Once they see evidence of success, reinforce the next step.

"Would it be useful if we scheduled a session to go over exactly how this would work for your team? That way, we can address any remaining concerns."

Exercise: Building Trust Through Proof

List three of your most compelling client success stories. Prepare a brief summary of each, focusing on the initial problem, the solution provided, and the measurable outcome.

Objection #20: *"This isn't a priority for us at the moment."*

Motive Behind It:

This objection often arises when the prospect does not **fully see the urgency** of your solution. The reasons could be:

- ✓ *They have more pressing business concerns.*
- ✓ *They don't fully recognize the impact of the problem your solution solves.*
- ✓ *They believe delaying the decision will not cause significant consequences.*

Handling This Objection Using the Four-Step Approach

Step 1: Acknowledge & Empathize

Rather than pushing back, recognize their current focus.

"I completely understand that your team has a lot on its plate. Many of our clients felt the same way when we first spoke."

Step 2: Ask & Clarify

To shift the conversation, ask about their current priorities.

"Out of curiosity, what are your biggest priorities right now? Often, our solution actually helps address some of those challenges."

Step 3: Address with Value

Connect your solution to their current priorities and highlight the **cost of inaction**.

"One of our clients, [Client Name], initially delayed implementing our solution for six months. Later, they found that the issue worsened, costing them [X amount in lost revenue/productivity]. When they finally adopted our solution, they wished they had done it sooner. Would it make sense to evaluate the long-term impact of waiting?"

Step 4: Confirm & Move Forward

Suggest a soft commitment.

"How about we schedule a follow-up in a month? That way, we can revisit this once you have more bandwidth."

Exercise: Defining the Cost of Inaction
For your solution, identify three risks of delaying a decision. Develop a brief narrative illustrating each risk.

Objection #21: *"Your solution doesn't integrate with our current systems."*
Motive Behind It:
The prospect fears that adopting your solution will cause **operational disruptions** or require costly infrastructure changes.
Handling This Objection Using the Four-Step Approach
Step 1: Acknowledge & Empathize
"That's a completely valid concern. No company wants to invest in a solution that disrupts existing workflows."
Step 2: Ask & Clarify
"What specific integrations are you looking for? Understanding that will help me see if we can provide a solution."
Step 3: Address with Value

- ✓ If your solution integrates:
  "Actually, our system does integrate with [specific software]. I can show you exactly how it works."
- ✓ If it doesn't integrate directly, explore workarounds:
  "While we don't have a native integration, many of our clients use [third-party tool] or a

simple API to connect our system. Would you be open to discussing how this could work?"

Step 4: Confirm & Move Forward

"How about a quick call with our technical team to explore your specific setup?"

Objection #22: *"We've already allocated our budget for the year."*

Motive Behind It:

The prospect is concerned about financial constraints and believes they cannot afford your solution until the next budgeting cycle.

Handling This Objection Using the Four-Step Approach

Step 1: Acknowledge & Empathize

"I completely understand. Budget constraints are a real challenge for many businesses."

Step 2: Ask & Clarify

"Since budgeting is planned in advance, are there discretionary funds available for high-priority projects?"

Step 3: Address with Value

- ✓ If flexibility is possible:
  "We offer flexible payment options that allow you to spread the cost over several months. Would that help?"
- ✓ If not, position future planning:
  "Many clients in your situation choose to start discussions now so they can secure budget allocation for next year. Would you be open to mapping out a plan?"

Step 4: Confirm & Move Forward

"Would you be open to a preliminary discussion with your finance team to explore options?"

Objection #23: *"I'm not the right person to discuss this."*

Motive Behind It:

The person you're speaking to may not have decision-making power, or they may be trying to end the conversation.

Handling This Objection Using the Four-Step Approach

Step 1: Acknowledge & Empathize

"I understand that decision-making often involves multiple people."

Step 2: Ask & Clarify

"Who in your organization would typically handle a decision like this?"

Step 3: Address with Value

"Would it be possible to set up a meeting with them? I can share relevant insights to help them evaluate this effectively."

Step 4: Confirm & Move Forward

"Can I send you some information to forward to the right person, or would you prefer an introduction call?"

Objection #24: *"We need more time to evaluate our options."*

Motive Behind It:

This objection often stems from either a genuine desire to compare solutions or an attempt to delay a decision. The prospect may:

- ✓ *Be unsure about committing and want more data.*
- ✓ *Have multiple stakeholders involved in the decision-making process.*
- ✓ *Be stalling because they are hesitant to make a change.*

Handling This Objection Systematically

The first step is to acknowledge their need for more time, rather than pushing them to act immediately.

"I completely understand that making an informed decision takes time, and I respect that. Many of our clients initially felt the same way."

To clarify their hesitation, ask a targeted question:

"What specific information are you still evaluating? Are there any concerns I can help address?"

If they are comparing multiple options, position your solution as uniquely valuable:

"Many of our customers were in a similar situation and found that our solution offered [key differentiator, e.g., better ROI, faster implementation, stronger support]. Would it help if I shared a case study or connected you with a customer who was in your position?"

Guide the next step:

"Since your team is still evaluating, how about we set up a follow-up call in two weeks? In the meantime, I can provide you with more detailed insights to help make the decision easier."

Exercise: Mapping the Competitor Comparison

List three unique selling points of your product compared to competitors. Prepare a way to present these insights compellingly during conversations.

Objection #25: *"Our company doesn't make quick decisions."*

Motive Behind It:

Large organizations often have lengthy decision-making processes, which may involve multiple stakeholders, legal approvals, or extended procurement cycles. The prospect may also be using this as an excuse to delay engagement.

Handling This Objection Systematically

Start by acknowledging the nature of their company's process:

"I completely understand that a structured decision-making process is essential, especially for a company of your size."

Rather than pushing for an immediate sale, ask:

"Could you walk me through how decisions like this are typically made in your organization? Understanding your process will help us provide the right support at the right time."

Once you know the timeline, suggest a way to align with it:

"Many of our clients with similar internal processes found it helpful to have an initial discussion now, so when the formal decision stage arrives, they already have the necessary details in place. Would that approach work for you?"

If they mention a specific timeframe, get a soft commitment:

"Would it make sense for us to schedule a check-in a month from now so we can ensure everything is aligned when the time comes?"

Objection #26: *"We're waiting for approval from higher-ups."*

Motive Behind It:

The prospect may not have the authority to make the decision or may be facing internal roadblocks. Sometimes, they are simply using this as a polite way to disengage.

Handling This Objection Systematically

Acknowledge their position:

"That makes perfect sense. In many organizations, key decisions require buy-in from multiple stakeholders."

Then, seek to understand the approval process:

"Would you be open to sharing what your leadership team typically looks for when evaluating solutions like this?"

If possible, offer to support them in the approval process:

"Would it be helpful if I provided a concise summary or ROI analysis that you could present to them?"

Finally, aim to engage the decision-makers directly:

"Would it be possible for us to set up a short call with your leadership team? That way, we can directly address any concerns they might have."

Objection #27: *"We had a bad experience with a similar product before."*

Motive Behind It:

This objection is rooted in past disappointment. The prospect may feel burned by a previous vendor and fear repeating the same mistake.

Handling This Objection Systematically

First, acknowledge their experience and build trust:

"I completely understand why you'd be hesitant after a previous bad experience. If I were in your position, I'd feel the same way."

Next, ask about the past failure:

"Would you mind sharing what specifically went wrong? That will help me determine if our solution is a better fit."

Once you identify the issue, address it head-on:

"From what you've shared, it sounds like the previous solution failed because of [specific issue]. Here's how we've addressed that in our approach…"

If applicable, share success stories:
"One of our current clients had the exact same concern. They had a poor experience with another vendor, but after switching to us, they saw [specific improvement]. Would you like to hear how they made that transition?"

Objection #28: *"We don't see a big enough problem to justify this purchase."*
Motive Behind It:
The prospect may not fully grasp the cost of inaction or the long-term benefits of your solution.
Handling This Objection Systematically
Begin by acknowledging their perspective:
"I appreciate that. Many businesses initially don't realize the impact until they dig deeper."
Ask a thought-provoking question:
"Would you mind if we explored how this challenge could evolve over time? Sometimes, the true cost isn't immediately obvious."
Illustrate the cost of inaction:
"One of our clients also thought they didn't have a big enough problem—until they lost [X amount] in missed opportunities. When they adopted our solution, they realized how much they had been leaving on the table."
Provide a low-risk way to test the value:
"Would you be open to a pilot program or a consultation to assess whether this would make a measurable difference for you?"

Objection #29: *"Your company is too new; we prefer established vendors."*
Motive Behind It:

The prospect fears that working with a newer company may come with risks like instability, lack of experience, or weak support.

Handling This Objection Systematically

Start by addressing their concern:

"I completely understand why you'd want to work with a well-established company. Reputation and stability matter."

Then, emphasize your strengths:

"While we may be newer, many of our customers have chosen us because we offer [specific advantage, e.g., cutting-edge technology, personalized support, faster innovation]."

Use social proof:

"We've already worked with companies like [Client Name], and they've seen [specific result]. Would you like to hear about their experience?"

Objection #30: *"We're not sure your company will be around long-term."*

Motive Behind It:

This objection stems from a fear of working with a company that may not be financially stable or have long-term viability.

Handling This Objection Systematically

Acknowledge their concern:

"I understand why longevity is important. No one wants to invest in a solution that won't be supported in the long run."

Reassure them:

"While we may not be the oldest company in the industry, we are backed by [funding, growth rate, strategic partnerships], which ensures our stability."

Provide proof of momentum:

"In the past [timeframe], we've expanded our customer base by [X%] and secured partnerships with [big-name clients]."

Offer reassurance through contract terms:

"We also offer long-term support guarantees. Would it help if I walked you through how that works?"

Advanced Strategies for Objection Handling

Handling objections effectively is a skill that separates top-performing sales professionals from the rest. It is not merely about overcoming resistance; it is about transforming skepticism into confidence, hesitation into action, and doubt into trust. In this chapter, we will explore advanced strategies that go beyond basic responses and help you turn objections into meaningful conversations that drive business growth.

Whether you are facing a price concern, skepticism about ROI, or reluctance due to internal decision-making barriers, these strategies will equip you with the tools to address objections with confidence, provide compelling proof, and build lasting customer relationships.

Using Data & Insights to Overcome Objections

Objections are often rooted in uncertainty. When prospects say, "We're not sure this will work for us," or "We don't see the ROI," what they are really expressing is a lack of clear evidence that justifies the investment. This is where data and insights become powerful tools.

The most effective way to handle these objections is to replace uncertainty with concrete facts, numbers, and projections that demonstrate the value of your solution.

For instance, imagine a prospect who is hesitant about switching from their existing supplier because they feel your offering is not significantly better. Instead of making vague claims, you could say:

"I completely understand that changing vendors is a big decision. Let me share something interesting—our customers, on average, see a 22% reduction in operational costs and a 30% improvement in efficiency after implementing our solution. In fact, one of our clients in your industry was in the same position and saved $50,000 annually. Would you like to see the breakdown of those savings?"

How to Use Data Effectively

- ✓ Use industry-specific benchmarks: If you can show that similar companies have gained measurable benefits, your prospect will be more inclined to trust your claims.
- ✓ Personalize the numbers: Instead of generic statistics, provide projections based on their company's data.
- ✓ Visualize the impact: Charts, graphs, and cost-benefit breakdowns help make the numbers more tangible.

Exercise:

- ✓ Identify three key objections your prospects frequently raise.
- ✓ Gather relevant statistics or case studies that address each of these objections.
- ✓ Prepare a visual slide or summary that presents this data concisely for your next sales call.

Leveraging Social Proof, Case Studies, and Testimonials

Social proof is one of the most persuasive tools in sales. When prospects hear that others like them have successfully used your product and achieved measurable results, their confidence in your solution increases.

For example, if a potential client says, "We're not sure your solution will integrate well with our current system," you could respond with:

"That's a great question! One of our customers, [Company Name], had the exact same concern. Initially, they were worried about compatibility, but after implementing our solution, they found that not only did it integrate seamlessly, but it also reduced manual work by 40%. Would you like to hear more about how they made the transition?"

How to Use Social Proof Effectively

- ✓ Choose case studies that align with the prospect's industry and pain points.
- ✓ Use direct quotes from satisfied customers. Real words from real clients carry more weight than general statements.
- ✓ Offer to connect prospects with happy customers so they can hear firsthand experiences.

Exercise:

- ✓ Gather 3-5 success stories from past clients.
- ✓ Create a "testimonial bank" with key quotes and statistics.
- ✓ Role-play a sales conversation where you introduce these success stories naturally.

Handling Objections Over Calls vs. Emails vs. In-Person Meetings

Sales objections can arise in different communication channels, and each medium requires a different approach.

Handling Objections Over Calls

Phone calls require quick thinking and real-time adaptability. Since you can hear the prospect's tone and hesitation, it is crucial to listen actively and respond with confidence.

For example, if a prospect says, "I need more time to think about it," you should avoid letting the conversation end there. Instead, dig deeper:

"I understand completely. Just to make sure I'm giving you the right information—what's the main factor you're considering right now?"

This keeps the conversation going and allows you to uncover the true hesitation.

Handling Objections Over Emails

Email objections tend to be more formal and brief. Since you lack verbal cues, your response must be clear, structured, and supported by data or social proof.

For example, if a prospect emails you saying, "We've decided to stay with our current provider," your response should:

Acknowledge their decision.

Offer a compelling reason to reconsider.

Suggest a follow-up discussion.

"I completely understand your decision, and I appreciate the time you've spent evaluating our solution. Before you finalize, I wanted to share a quick insight—companies that switched to us reported an average of 25% higher efficiency in their first six months. Would it be worth a 15-minute chat to see if these benefits could apply to your team?"

Handling Objections In-Person

Face-to-face meetings provide the best opportunity to build rapport and read body language. When handling objections in person, it's effective to:

- ✓ Use visual aids (charts, customer stories, demos).

- ✓ Ask deeper questions to address unspoken concerns.
- ✓ Suggest a next step that keeps the conversation open.

Exercise:

Practice responding to a common objection over a call, email, and in-person meeting.

Compare how your approach differs in each scenario.

Negotiation Techniques to Turn Objections into Opportunities

Objections are not always roadblocks—they can be stepping stones to negotiation. A skilled salesperson can turn concerns into discussions that ultimately lead to a deal.

For example, if a prospect says, "Your competitor is offering a better price," instead of immediately lowering your price, you can reframe the conversation:

"I understand that pricing is an important factor. But let me ask—beyond price, what matters most to your team? Is it customer support, long-term cost savings, or ease of use?"

This shifts the focus from cost alone to overall value. Once the prospect acknowledges other important factors, you can highlight why your solution is superior.

Key Negotiation Strategies

- ✓ Ask open-ended questions to uncover their true priorities.
- ✓ Offer flexible terms (e.g., trial periods, phased implementation).
- ✓ Frame pricing as an investment, not an expense.

Exercise:

- ✓ Write down a recent sales objection you faced.
- ✓ Identify 2-3 negotiation tactics you could have used to shift the conversation.
- ✓ Role-play the revised conversation with a colleague.

Building Long-Term Relationships with Customers Who Objected Before

Not every prospect will buy immediately. However, *a "no" today doesn't mean a "no" forever.* Many of your best customers may have initially objected but later came back when the timing was right.

The key is consistent, value-driven follow-ups.

For example, if a prospect said, "We don't have the budget for this right now," you can check in months later with a relevant industry update:

"Hey [Prospect's Name], I remember our conversation about [challenge]. I just came across this new research showing how companies in your industry are solving this issue, and I thought of you. Would love to hear your thoughts!"

This keeps the relationship warm without feeling pushy.

Best Practices for Long-Term Follow-Ups

- ✓ Follow up with insights, not just sales pitches.
- ✓ Stay connected through LinkedIn and industry events.
- ✓ Celebrate their company's wins (e.g., a LinkedIn comment on their achievements).

Exercise:

- ✓ Identify 3 past prospects who objected.
- ✓ Draft a follow-up message that provides value rather than asking for a sale.

- ✓ Send those messages today.

Objection handling is not about overcoming resistance—it's about building trust. When you approach objections with a mindset of education, problem-solving, and long-term value, you turn potential rejections into lasting customer relationships.

Final Tips & Best Practices

Objection handling is not a one-time skill that you master and forget. It is a dynamic process that requires continuous improvement, customization, and practice. The best sales professionals don't just react to objections; they anticipate them, refine their responses, and use every challenge as an opportunity to build stronger relationships.

In this final section, we will explore four crucial aspects of mastering objection handling: developing a personal playbook, practicing through role-play, continuously refining your approach, and learning how top sales professionals turn objections into sales.

By the time you finish this chapter, you will have a system in place that will allow you to confidently handle any sales objection, improve your sales conversations, and close more deals.

Developing a Personal Objection-Handling Playbook – Customizing Responses Based on Your Industry

Sales objections are rarely generic. While some concerns are universal—such as pricing, trust, or timing—many objections are specific to the industry, company size, decision-making process, and even cultural factors.

For instance, if you are selling enterprise software, objections often revolve around integration challenges, data security, and long approval cycles. **If you are selling** manufacturing equipment, concerns might be operational downtime, long-term ROI, and supply chain reliability.

Instead of relying on generic responses, the best salespeople create a personalized playbook that addresses the most common objections in their industry.

How to Build Your Own Objection-Handling Playbook

Start by listing the **10-15 most frequent objections** you hear from prospects. For each objection, break it down into:

- ✓ **The real underlying concern behind the objection.**
  For example, when a prospect says, *"This is too expensive,"* are they really concerned about price, or are they unsure about the value your solution provides?
- ✓ **A customized response that is relevant to your industry.**
  If you're in SaaS sales, your response might highlight long-term cost savings compared to in-house development. If you're in healthcare sales, you might emphasize compliance and efficiency.
- ✓ **Real-life success stories and data points to back up your response.**
  Instead of just saying, *"Our solution will save you money,"* show how another customer reduced costs by 30% after implementing your product.
- ✓ **A follow-up strategy for overcoming persistent concerns.**
  Not all objections disappear immediately. If a prospect is skeptical, what follow-up emails, demo sessions, or case studies can you send to reinforce your value proposition?

Example: Industry-Specific Response to an Objection

Objection: *"We don't have the budget for this right now."*

Industry: HR & Talent Acquisition Software

Response:

"I completely understand that budgets are tight, especially in today's economy. Many of our clients initially had the same concern. But when they looked at how much they were spending on manual recruitment processes—hiring agencies, job board fees, and lost productivity—they realized that our software actually saved them money in the long run. In fact, [Client Name] reduced their cost-per-hire by 35% in just six months. Would you like to see how this could apply to your team?"

Exercise:

- ✓ Take the top five objections you hear in your industry.
- ✓ Write a detailed response for each, including a real customer story or data point.
- ✓ Practice delivering these responses naturally in a conversation.

Role-Playing & Practicing Objection Handling – Exercises for Sales Teams

Just like athletes train before a big game, sales professionals need consistent practice to master objection handling. Role-playing is one of the most effective ways to develop confidence, refine responses, and prepare for real-world objections.

How to Conduct Effective Objection-Handling Role-Plays

- ✓ Pair up with a colleague and take turns playing the prospect and the salesperson. The person acting as the prospect should present a realistic objection, while the salesperson must respond naturally.

- ✓ Use real case scenarios from past sales conversations. If your team frequently hears objections about implementation difficulties, practice responses tailored to that issue.
- ✓ Record your role-play sessions and analyze them. Are you using clear, confident language? Are you responding with value-driven statements rather than just countering objections?
- ✓ Gradually introduce more challenging objections. Start with common objections like budget concerns, then move to tougher ones like internal bureaucracy, past bad experiences, or competition.

Example Role-Playing Exercise

Scenario: A prospect says, *"We're interested, but we need more time to evaluate our options."*

Step 1: One salesperson acts as the prospect, presenting the objection naturally.
Step 2: The other salesperson responds, asking clarifying questions and handling the objection.
Step 3: The team gives feedback on what worked well and what could be improved.
Step 4: Repeat the exercise, refining the response based on feedback.

Exercise:

- ✓ Conduct three different role-play sessions this week, each focusing on a different objection.
- ✓ Identify areas for improvement and adjust your objection-handling strategies accordingly.

Continuous Learning: Monitoring & Improving Your Approach

Sales is an evolving profession. What works today might not work tomorrow, especially as market trends, customer behaviors, and competitive landscapes shift.

Top sales professionals constantly refine their strategies by:

- ✓ Tracking which objections come up most frequently. If you notice that pricing objections are increasing, is it a sign that competitors are offering better value? If integration concerns are common, should you work more closely with your product team to address them?
- ✓ Recording and analyzing sales calls. Reviewing past conversations helps identify areas where you could have responded more effectively.
- ✓ Learning from top performers. Study how the best salespeople on your team handle objections. What phrases do they use? How do they reframe conversations?
- ✓ Staying updated on industry trends. The more knowledge you have about your market, the more confidently you can handle objections. Attend industry events, read reports, and follow thought leaders in your space.

Exercise:

- ✓ Review your last five sales calls or meetings.
- ✓ Identify one objection you struggled with and rewrite a better response.
- ✓ Use that improved response in your next call.

How Top Sales Professionals Turn Objections into Sales

The best salespeople don't fear objections; they welcome them. They know that when a prospect raises an objection, it means they are engaged and considering the purchase. The real danger is when a prospect is indifferent and doesn't engage at all.

What Sets Top Sales Professionals Apart?

- ✓ They ask deeper questions. Instead of rushing to counter an objection, they explore the underlying concern.
- ✓ They focus on value, not just price. Instead of discounting their solution, they show how it will save money or generate higher ROI.
- ✓ They handle objections with confidence, not defensiveness. A great salesperson never sounds nervous or uncertain when faced with an objection.
- ✓ They use objections as an opportunity to strengthen relationships. Instead of pushing a sale, they offer insights, share relevant case studies, and position themselves as trusted advisors.

Example: Reframing an Objection into a Sales Opportunity

- ✓ Prospect: *"We're happy with our current provider."*
- ✓ Top Salesperson's Response: *"That's great to hear! That means you already see the value in a solution like ours. Out of curiosity, if there were one thing you could improve about your current provider, what would it be?"*

This approach keeps the conversation open and encourages the prospect to reveal potential pain points.

Exercise:

- ✓ Think of an objection that recently prevented a sale.
- ✓ How could you have reframed the conversation to turn it into an opportunity?
- ✓ Write down your new approach and try it in your next sales call.

Mastering objection handling requires customization, practice, continuous learning, and a mindset shift. By applying the strategies in this chapter, you will not only overcome objections but also build deeper trust with prospects and increase your close rate.
Which strategy will you start implementing today?

Conclusion

Mastering the art of handling objections is one of the most valuable skills a sales professional can develop. It separates average salespeople from top performers. Those who embrace objections, understand the psychology behind them, and respond strategically are the ones who not only close more deals but also build lasting relationships with clients.

Throughout this handbook, we have explored a structured, strategic approach to objection handling. We started by understanding why objections arise—whether they stem from real concerns, internal roadblocks, or even hesitation masked as skepticism. We then moved through a step-by-step process to break down objections, address them confidently, and guide prospects toward a positive buying decision.

As we conclude, let's revisit the key takeaways from this handbook and offer some final thoughts on mastering objection handling.

Key Takeaways from the Handbook

One of the most important realizations about objections is that they are **not** roadblocks; they are stepping stones to deeper conversations. When a prospect raises an objection, it's an opportunity to uncover their real concerns, demonstrate value, and differentiate yourself from the competition.

Objections Are a Natural Part of the Sales Process

If a prospect is engaging with you and raising objections, they are **not** rejecting you outright—they are considering their options. A lack of objections should worry you more than an abundance of them. It may indicate that the prospect is not truly interested or invested in the conversation.

For example, imagine you are selling a marketing automation platform, and a prospect says, *"We don't have the budget for this right now."* Instead of assuming the conversation is over, a great salesperson sees this as a chance to ask, *"I completely understand. Can I ask what your marketing team's biggest challenge is right now?"* This keeps the conversation open and allows you to pivot towards discussing ROI rather than just cost.

Handling Objections Requires Preparation, Not Just Improvisation

Many salespeople make the mistake of waiting until an objection comes up to think about how to handle it. Top sales professionals, on the other hand, prepare in advance by creating a personal objection-handling playbook.

For instance, if you frequently encounter the objection, *"We already have a similar solution,"* having a well-rehearsed response can help. A top sales rep might respond with:

"That's great to hear! Many of our customers were using other solutions before switching to us. Just out of curiosity, what do you like most about your current solution, and is there anything you wish was better?"

This response keeps the conversation open and allows you to find gaps where your solution might be a better fit.

Objections Are Often Emotional, Not Just Logical

While some objections are based on concrete factors like budget limitations or technical requirements, many objections are rooted in fear, skepticism, or hesitation. Understanding the emotional drivers behind objections is key to handling them effectively.

For example, if a prospect says, *"We had a bad experience with a similar product before,"* their real concern isn't just about the product itself—it's about avoiding another disappointment. Instead of immediately defending your solution, you might respond with:

"I completely understand. Could you tell me more about what happened? I want to make sure we don't repeat any of those mistakes and that our solution truly meets your needs."

By acknowledging their concerns and showing empathy, you build trust, which is often the missing ingredient in closing deals.

The Best Salespeople Anticipate and Preempt Objections

Instead of waiting for objections to arise, top sales professionals bring them up proactively **and** address them before the prospect even mentions them.

For instance, if you know that a common objection in your industry is *"Your company is too new; we prefer established vendors,"* you can preemptively address this by saying:

"I know some companies worry about working with a newer provider, but what many of our customers have found is that because we are newer, we are also more agile and responsive. In fact, we've helped companies like [Client Name] implement our solution faster than traditional providers because of our hands-on approach. Would it be helpful if I shared their case study with you?"

By bringing up the objection before they do, you demonstrate confidence, transparency, and credibility.

Handling Objections Is About Building Long-Term Relationships, Not Just Closing Sales

One of the most important shifts in mindset is seeing objections as a chance to build relationships rather than just a hurdle to overcome. Not every prospect will buy from you immediately, but how you handle their objections can determine whether they return to you in the future.

For example, if a prospect says, *"We're not ready to make a decision yet,"* a short-term-minded salesperson might move on and forget about them. A relationship-focused salesperson, on the other hand, might say:

"That makes perfect sense. Many of our best clients took some time to evaluate their options before moving forward. If it's helpful, I can send you some industry insights and updates over the next few months so you stay informed. Would that be valuable for you?"

This approach keeps the door open and positions you as a trusted advisor rather than just a salesperson.

Final Thoughts on Mastering the Art of Handling Objections

Objection handling is both a science and an art. The science lies in understanding the common objections, preparing structured responses, and using data to support your claims. The art is in how you deliver your response—your tone, timing, confidence, and ability to adapt in real time.

Great sales professionals don't fear objections—they welcome them. Every objection is a signal of interest, a chance to understand the prospect better, and an opportunity to provide clarity and reassurance.

A Personal Challenge for You

To truly master objection handling, it's not enough to just read about it. You have to practice it daily. Here's a challenge for you:

- ✓ Choose one objection that you struggle with the most.
- ✓ Write down a new response that is more strategic, engaging, and value-driven.
- ✓ Practice delivering it out loud until it feels natural.
- ✓ Use it in your next sales call and observe the difference.

The Path to Becoming a Sales Expert

Sales is a journey of continuous improvement. The best salespeople don't stop refining their skills just because they close a deal. They analyze their conversations, learn from every interaction, and seek out ways to get better every single day.

If you commit to applying the principles in this handbook, you will not only handle objections more effectively, **but you will also** build deeper relationships, close more deals, and establish yourself as a top sales professional in your industry.

Your Next Steps

- ✓ Start building your personal objection-handling playbook based on real conversations.
- ✓ Practice role-playing objections with colleagues or mentors.
- ✓ Continuously analyze and refine your responses after each sales conversation.
- ✓ Never stop learning—every objection is a chance to grow.

With the right mindset and strategies, objections are not obstacles; they are the bridge to closing more deals and building lasting customer relationships.
So, the next time you hear an objection, don't back away—lean in, listen deeply, and turn it into an opportunity.
This is what separates great sales professionals from the rest. Are you ready to take your sales skills to the next level?

About the Author
'GERARD ASSEY'

Gerard Assey is a Graduate in Economics, a PGD in Management (HRD) and holds a Doctorate in Leadership. Gerard holds several International Qualifications in Sales, Debt Collection, Training & Teaching, and is a 'Fellow' of the prestigious 'Institute of Sales & Marketing Management'-UK, a Certified NLP Practitioner, a 'Certified Trainer', an 'Accredited Management Teacher-Behavioral Sciences', a 'Certified Competency Facilitator', a 'Certified Management Consultant'- (the International credentials of a professional management consultant, awarded in accordance with global standards of the ICMCI); and a Certification from the University of Michigan in 'Successful Negotiation: Essential Strategies and Skills'

He is also a Member of the 'National Association of Sales Professionals' backed with several years experience in varied industries, both in India and Overseas. He also holds an 'Etiquette Consultant' Certification from the USA (by Sue Fox, Author of Best Seller: 'Business Etiquette for Dummies'. She has trained some of the top celebrities' world over). He was also a recipient of a scholarship for extensive training in Japan on 'Corporate Management for India'.

Gerard Assey is 'Founder & Chief Corporate Trainer' of the Group: '**Citius, Altius, Fortius Unlimited'**- an organization that **celebrated 20 years of Glorious Service** in 2021, focusing on 3 Core Competencies:

People. Performance. Profit; in functional areas of Sales & Marketing, HR & Organizational Development, covering Recruitment, Training & Consultancy!

Having managed organizations with large Sales Forces in India & Overseas, his specialization cover extensive areas of Sales Training (All levels - Presentation, Negotiation, Key/ Strategic Accounts Management & Managerial Skills for all sectors), Bid Proposal/ Capture Planning/ Management Trainings, Retail Sales, Customer Service & Customer Retention Programs, Training for Prevention & Collection of Debt, Self & Personal Development Programs (Time Management, Teamwork & Team Building, Business Etiquette & Personal Grooming, Leadership & Managerial Skills, People Management Skills, Train-the-Trainer etc), including preparation of Custom-designed Business Manuals for Internal (HR, Induction, and Sales etc) & External use (Instruction, User Manuals).

Gerard has successfully conducted over 6440 Trainings & Workshops (as of Mar '25) all across India, Middle East, Africa, Europe & S.E. Asia. Besides public programs conducted regularly, both in India & Overseas, he has some of the top names as clients whom he services from Single Owners to large Public & Government undertakings, covering all sectors, for their in-house needs.

His website: www.CollectionSkills.com is the only one in this part of the world to be featured in the 'Collections & Credit Risk Magazine-USA' under 'Who's Who in Training' and ranks TOP, along with other websites listed below on most search engines.

Gerard is author of 178 books already (Mar 2025), all the books being available on all online platforms and outlets as E-books and Paperbacks

A few of our business related books:

1. Bite-sized Bits on Commonsense Management
2. Heart to Heart on Life's Principles'
3. How to become a Successful Manager
4. The Sales Professionals' Master Workbook of S.Y.S.T.E.M.S
5. The Professional Business Email Etiquette Handbook & Guide
6. The Professional Business Video-Conferencing Etiquette Handbook & Guide
7. Professional Presentation Skills
8. Exceptional Customer Service
9. Professional Tele-Marketing Skills
10. Professional Debt Collection Skills
11. The G.R.E.A.T. Sales & Service Workbook
12. Sales Training Advantage for Results (*The Ultimate Sales Training Manual to enable you stand out as a S.T.A.R.*)
13. CEO Daily Planner & Organizer
14. The Sales Professionals' Master Daily Planner
15. The Professional Debt Collector's Master Daily Planner
16. My Daily Planner & Organizer
17. MY EMERGENCY INFORMATION RECORD (Family Emergency & Peace of Mind Planner)
18. The Ultimate Therapist & Counselors Planner and Organizer
19. Building an Ethical Workplace
20. Managing Relationships at Work
21. Managing Business Meetings Effectively
22. Effective Delegation Skills
23. Goal Setting for Success
24. B2B Selling by Email
25. Professional Business Etiquette & Grooming
26. Dining Etiquette & Table Manners
27. Effective Networking Skills
28. Grooming, Etiquette & Manners for Teens, Young Adults & Future Leaders
29. Inter-Personal Skills
30. Get Ready, Get Hired!
31. Selling in a Recession

32. Effective Receivables Management in an Economic Downturn!
33. Real Estate & Property Sales Training
34. Credit Sales & Accounts Receivable Management
35. Selling Skills for Real Estate & Property Advisors
36. Take G.R.E.A.T. C.A.R.E!
37. Spa, Salon & Health Club Selling Skills
38. Selling Travel, Holiday & MICE Services
39. Selling Skills for Spa's, Salons & Health Clubs
40. Retailing in Salons & Spas
41. Selling Holiday, Vacation, Tours & Packages
42. The Power of Sales Referrals
43. Selling Luxury
44. Technical Selling Skills
45. Financial Advisors Sales Training
46. Dealing with Burnout at Work Monopolize Your Markets
47. Selling to Affluent Customers
48. Growing up with Grace
49. Financial Selling Skills
50. *The Effective Manager's Guide: Key Skills to Thrive*
51. From Aspiring to Inspiring: A Guide for New Managers on the Rise
52. The Power of Focus
53. Selling with Integrity: Sell Like Jesus The Perfect Role Model!
54. 31 Habits of Champions: Your 31-Day Journey to Greatness
55. Rejecting Grasshopper Talk: From Grasshopper to Giant-Killer-*Defeating Giants Daily!*
56. Navigate the AI-Powered Future of Bid & Proposals: Up-Skill to Stay Relevant with Alternative Career Paths & Opportunities
57. Hiring Sales Winners
58. Present with Impact
59. Success Unlocked: *Breaking Free from Habits that Hold You Back*
60. Complaints to Cheers, Feedback to Gold: Mastering Complaints Management
61. Thriving Together: *Cultivating Diversity, Equity, and Inclusion*
62. Coaching Skills for Sales Managers

63. Soaring to Success in Business & Leadership: Swifter, Higher, Stronger!
64. From Classroom to Podium: A Student's Guide to Powerful Public Speaking & Presentation Skills
65. Developing Self-Discipline
66. The CEO's 31-Day Power Plan: Unlocking Success through Essential Traits
67. Credibility Matters
68. A Winning Attitude
69. Bid & Proposal Management Using AI
70. Sales Forecasting: A Practical & Proven Guide to Strategic Sales Forecasting
71. Elevate & Energize: *50 Dynamic & Fun Activities for Peak Workplace Morale*
72. 'Sales SOS! Sales on Fire! *30 Days to Conquer Chaos & the Nightmares of Success!'*
73. Mastering Sales Managerial Skills: *Building High-Performing Teams & Driving Exceptional Results*
74. Eagle-Eyed Leadership: Unleashing the Power of 31 Lessons from Eagles
75. The Ultimate Employee Training Guide: *Training Today, Leading Tomorrow*
76. Being More Accountable at Work
77. Creating a Culture of Continuous Improvement
78. Effective Questioning & Listening Skills
79. The Power of Value Selling
80. The Growth Mindset
81. Mastering Professional Help Desk Skills
82. The Power to Lead with Empathy
83. Being Prepared: The Key to Unlocking Success
84. Youthful Spark-Youth Energizers, Activities and Games-Igniting the Fun in Youth
85. Ignite your Motivation for Success
86. Elevate Your Executive Presence: *Your Roadmap to Executive Excellence*
87. Smart Decisions: *Mastering Problem Solving with Strategic Solutions for Business Success*
88. Strategic Planning: *Developing and Implementing Strategic Plans to Achieve Long-Term Business Goals*
89. The Power of Stay Interviews
90. Developing G.R.I.T.
91. Adaptability

92. Diagnosis- *A Key Skill for Leadership*
93. The Burnout-Proof Salesperson: *The Master Guide to Preventing Stress & Burnout-* Strategies for Thriving in Sales
94. Learning from Failure: *Keys to Success*
95. Customer Success Management
96. Overcoming the Killers of Motivation
97. The C-Suite Code: *Mastering Skills for Executive Excellence'*
98. Dealing with Difficult Customers
99. Unlocking Your Potential: Mastering the Top 20 Life Skills for a Brighter Future
100. Nurturing Tomorrow's Leaders: *Essential Soft Skills Every Child Must Learn*
101. Lively & Fun Party Games for Seniors & Elders
102. Role Playing for Sales Champions: From Practice to Performance
103. Fun and Exciting Party Games for Kids
104. Case Studies for Sales
105. Role-Playing for Unbeatable Customer Service
106. Case Studies in Customer Service
107. Case Studies in Winning Negotiations
108. Case Studies in Management & Leadership
109. Case Studies in Human Resources & Talent Management
110. CEO Success Blueprint: The Essential Toolkit for CEOs and C-Level Executives
111. The Salesperson's Self-Coaching Guide: *Master Your Own Self-Coaching Plan for Success*
112. Overcoming Procrastination: *Your Ultimate Guide to Stop Delaying and Start Living Your Best Life*
113. When True Colors Are Exposed: *The Journey to Unmasking Humanity*
114. Life-Changing Habits for Teens: Teen Success Blueprint for a Bright Future
115. Workplace Stress-Free: *Proven Strategies to Thrive at Work and Beyond*
116. Objection Overruled: *The Ultimate Guide to Turning 'No' into 'Yes'"*

Besides regularly contributing to business & trade journals, including international ones such as the 'Creative Training Techniques' and the 'Sales News' of the U.S.A, He is also a member of several prestigious bodies & trade associations, having participated in many Conferences & Workshops in India & Overseas.

Prior to his last assignment of leading & managing a large MNC as head, Gerard had a 3-year stint in the Middle East as a Consultant with a leading British Consultancy Firm.

As the past 'Official Country Representative' for the International Business Award- 'THE STEVIES'-(the business world's own Oscar) for about 4 years- he ensured a few Indian companies that qualify for the same every year!

Gerard can be contacted at:
Email: training@Sales-Training.in,training@CollectionSkills.com
Websites:

www.Sales-Training.in
www.EtiquetteWorks.in
www.CollectionSkills.com
www.RetailSalesTraining.in
www.SalesTrainingIndia.com
www.ManualPreparation.com
www.TrainingWithPuppets.com
www.FirstContactAcademy.com
www.SalesAndMarketingRecruiter.com

Our TRAININGS that can help your team

- ✓ **Sales Effectiveness**: Selling Skills for any Sector: Service/ Logistics/ FMCG Realty/ Insurance & Finance/ Media/ SPA's, Health Clubs & Salons/ Key Account Management, Effective Negotiation Skills/ Bid & Proposal Management Skills/ Retail Sales Training: Any Sector (Auto, Jewelry, Clothing, Luxury etc)
- ✓ **Customer Service Skills**-Complaints Handling & Customer Retention
- ✓ **Debt Prevention & Collection Skills**
- ✓ **Etiquette & Grooming**
- ✓ **Leadership & Managerial Skills**
- ✓ **Self & Personal Development Skills**: Presentation Skills/ Effective Communication Skills/Business Proposal Writing Skills/ Problem Solving & Decision Making Skills/ Empowering Secretaries-The perfect PA! (For Secretaries & PA's)/ Effective Time Management/ Teamwork & Teambuilding/ P.R.I.D.E- **P**ersonal **R**esponsibility **I**n **D**elivering **E**xcellence

www.ingramcontent.com/pod-product-compliance
Ingram Content Group UK Ltd.
Pitfield, Milton Keynes, MK11 3LW, UK
UKHW021341190726
13845UKWH00027B/659

9 788198 569141